crème BRÛLÉE

THE BONJOUR WAY RECIPES BY RANDOLPH W. MANN

{ america's favorite dessert }

BONJOUR.

contents

a crème brûlée for all seasons

where and when crème brûlée was born is not 100% certain, but Britain, France, and Spain all lay claim to it. Regardless of its origin, the popularity of Crème Brûlée clearly extends as far back as the 17th Century. In English, it was originally known as "Burnt Cream," and the French "Crème Brûlée" carries the same literal meaning. Although the translation does little to stimulate our sweet tooth, the French does at least sound as romantic as our associations with this dreamy dessert. One thing is for sure — by any name, it grows more and more popular all the time and has already stood up well for 400 years. Anyone who has used a spoon to break through the crackling, glass-like caramelized surface to scoop up a mouthful of the ever so soft custard knows why.

some desserts are worth investing in special equipment for. Crème Brûlée, which has now surpassed chocolate mousse on the popularity charts, is certainly one of these. Surprisingly, not much paraphernalia is needed at all, but for caramelizing the crunchy top, a convenient culinary torch is essential for the serious enthusiast. Other than that, right-sized ramekins are a good idea to ensure perfect baking. Just having the right tools makes Crème Brûlée a breeze. Though extremely elegant, it is one of the simplest desserts when one has good equipment to work with.

just 30 years ago, Americans sat down to watch TV in the evening and saw their favorite chef, Julia Child, making Crème Brûlée at home for the very first time. Up until that moment, most Americans had barely heard of the delicacy, unless they were fortunate enough to have traveled in France. Julia had no problem with making and chilling the custard. The real challenge came when she had to run a 30-foot hose from the propane tank in her garage to her kitchen counter where, with a less than fashionable welder's mask, she caramelized the sugar to a golden color in seconds. America was never to forget its dramatic introduction to this awesome dessert, yet even Julia would be sure to agree that time has brought welcome changes. Luckily, torches of today, like those made by BonJour, provide a simple way to enjoy this crowd-pleasing treat anytime at home.

perhaps its widespread appeal accounts for the variations that spring up endlessly. After all, could we find anything better than cream to pair up with chocolate, nuts, fruit, and caramel? What's more, it's just as easy to add cream to our favorite liqueurs as it is to marry it with seasonal holiday favorites like pumpkin and cranberries.

the evolution of crème brûlée has come full circle. It began as a common dessert that was easily made by home cooks. Then, for a long time, because of its mystique of seeming complexity, crème brûlée became a specialty, attempted only by great chefs in posh restaurants. Now, with amazing speed, this simple dessert is once again becoming part of the repertoire of adventurous cooks in home kitchens across the land. The availability of affordable, simple-to-use equipment, like the BonJour Crème Brûlée Set, is certainly "heating up" the trend. What's more, the needed basic ingredients — cream, milk, eggs, sugar, and vanilla — are almost always found in anyone's kitchen.

all who use this book should be prepared for a journey of delight — joy in the culinary process and equal delight for those who will sample the results. May you be one of the cooks who will extend the great heritage and history of Crème Brûlée for future generations. Bon Voyage and Bon Appetit!

getting geared up

To get started on the right foot and to know the satisfaction of great results, it's important to have the few tools essential for this endeavor and all the proper ingredients:

the bonjour cooking torch

Made especially for crème brûlée, it is the single most needed specialty item that will consistently let you enjoy results that are exceptional instead of just acceptable. It has features to make it as safe as it is convenient — its anti-flare flame, safety lock, removable stand, adjustable flame, and easy to fill port. Because the torches in the BonJour line are lightweight and ergonomically designed, they allow you to make restaurant-quality desserts at home. The ideal is to caramelize the top of the crème brûlée without heating up the custard filling below, and this torch accomplishes just that.

Butane fuel can be purchased in small cans that insert in the bottom of the torch for effortless fueling. The best part is that one fueling can last for hours.

Surprisingly, even when you're not making crème brûlée, you're going to find a large number of other uses for the cooking torch in the kitchen — browning meringues, melting cheese atop onion soup, quick-roasting peppers and tomatoes — just to name a few. For more great ideas, see pages 48–49.

ramekins

To make most of the basic, 4-serving recipes in this book, a set of four (4-ounce) ramekins will be essential. Those with the shallow, oval design cook quickly and evenly. For larger parties, you'll want two or more sets. Recipes for four can always be doubled with no change in quality. Recipes for eight can always be cut in half.

For certain specialty crème brûlées, deep, round 4-ounce ramekins or custard cups can be beneficial.

a hot water bath

The hot water bath provides a gentle, even distribution of heat so the filling cooks uniformly and keeps the smoothest possible texture. Increased humidity from the bath also helps to prevent a thick skin from forming on the surface of the creamy custard.

Sometimes referred to as the French "bain-marie," it is made with a baking pan large enough to hold all of your ramekins. When the filling is ready to be baked, place the ramekins in the baking pan, fill them with the custard mixture, and then carefully pour very hot tap water or boiling water into the pan around them so that it comes about half way up their sides. Some people prefer to place the bain-marie on the oven rack before filling with hot water.

Is it necessary to cover the hot water bath while baking? This is a controversial point, but if you do decide to do so, cover very loosely with a sheet of foil. Crème brûlée recipes in this book are all designed to bake at 300° F, a temperature that doesn't create a thick skin on the custards. The down-side of covering is that water droplets can sometimes form under the cover and drip into the custard. Try to tent so this is less likely to happen.

When placing the hot water bath in the oven and when taking it out, it is important to move slowly and carefully so as not to slosh water into the custard. For this reason, a baking pan with handles can provide more stability and make carrying easier. For certain recipes, the ramekins will be left in the water bath to cool on the counter after baking.

other cookware and utensils

In some cases, a double boiler will be necessary to provide gentle stovetop heat, especially for stovetop, stirred crème brûlée. Make sure the top of the double boiler does not actually touch the water in the pot below.

For the purpose of heating cream and melting chocolate choose a fairly heavy saucepan to minimize the possibility of scorching. Non-stick cookware has its advantages in this situation. Many cooks find glass measuring cups and bowls efficient because they can be used to heat cream and melt chocolate in the microwave and have the added advantage of pouring well when it comes to filling the ramekins.

Though an electric beater is ideal for meringues, a small whisk will be indispensable for the crème brûlée when blending egg yolks with the other ingredients.

A fine strainer is used to remove spices, fruit pulp, and bits of coagulated egg so that the smoothest of custards can be achieved.

ingredients

As you know, the basic crème brûlée is a magical transformation of the simplest ingredients into a world-class marvel, but choosing the best raw materials is paramount.

cream: In the dairy section of most grocery stores, you can always find an array of pasteurized cream products. From lightest to richest butterfat content, the most common are: Half-and-half, light cream (also called light whipping cream), whipping cream, heavy whipping cream, country-style whipping cream, and double cream. Any cream will work as long as you have at least 2 egg yolks per cup of cream. However, the richness will be different, depending on which you choose to use. If a crème brûlée is to contain rich caramel and chocolate, it might be good to choose a light cream. The biggest concern should be the purity of the cream. It is a good idea to avoid those that contain added dextrose, carrageenan, mono and diglycerides, cellulose gum, and polysorbate 80. Look for one in which the only ingredient is **cream.**

milk: Sometimes a small percentage of milk is used to provide a lighter taste or to keep the custard from thickening too much. Choose whole milk unless you have need to severely restrict calories.

eggs: Always use "Grade A Large" or "Grade A Extra Large." Since the eggs are the only binder, using smaller eggs could result in a custard that won't set up enough. Used directly from the refrigerator, they will separate easier.

sugar: Granulated sugar and light brown sugar work fine, as is, for the custard mixture, but for caramelizing on top, sometimes a mixture of dried brown sugar and granulated sugar can produce a more flavorful dessert. See "Making Special Brûlée Sugar," page 8. Never try to torch artificial sugars, but they will produce fair results in the custard itself.

spices: You should infuse the cream with spices during the scalding process and allow them to remain in the cream until it has cooled for more then 10 minutes. If you have time to wait, 25 minutes will be better. Crème brûlée can be flavored with any spice you choose to use, even if it is dried vegetable matter like chipotle pepper or flowers like edible-grade lavender and roses.

fruit: Of course, any fruit can be added on top of the cooked crème brûlée, but if you intend to add it to the custard before baking, it is important to consider the moisture content of the fruit and how much of it will be released during baking. Dried fruits work very well, as do bananas and most blueberries.

liquid essences and liqueurs: If 3 egg yolks are used per cup of cream, up to an additional tablespoon of liqueur or essence may be added without making the custard too soft. Think of how much fun one could have experimenting with all of the wonderful liqueurs that pair well with cream.

salt: Just a pinch, and no more than a pinch, will spark all the flavors and accentuate the sweetness, even if you decrease the amount of sugar that is called for.

procedures: tips and techniques

the oven

A 300-degree oven is used consistently because it almost guarantees crème brûlée that sets with a fragile, creamy texture and does not brown on the top. It is also important that your oven rack be placed one notch below the middle of the oven. This will make sure that the tops remain totally soft and pliable. If you are not sure that your oven heats accurately, invest in an oven thermometer. They are economical and essential for the success of this delicate dessert. The oven must be exact.

scalding cream and milk

Traditionally, this is done on stovetop in a saucepan or double boiler. If just cream is used, you can actually bring it to the boiling point, but if milk is added to the cream, do not allow it to boil. Great results can also be achieved in the microwave in proper glass utensils, if done with periodic stirring and a watchful eye. No need to worry about the skin that forms on the top of the cream as it cools. That will be strained out.

infusions

For crème brûlée, the most delicate flavor will be achieved by adding whole spices or zests to the cream during the scalding process. Then the spices and cream should be allowed to steep from 10 to 30 minutes. Go right ahead and mix the spices and cream with all other ingredients. The spices will be strained out later.

mixing and tempering egg yolks

In most of the crème brûlée recipes, egg yolks are combined with the sugar and hot or warm cream is added later. When mixing the yolks and sugar, do not beat. It will incorporate too much air which will remain as bubbles on top of the baked custards. Instead, mix briskly in a circular motion until well blended. In the case of adding hot cream to the yolk mixture, add very small amounts at first and be sure to keep stirring vigorously all the time. Do not add all of the hot cream at once. Bring the temperature of the yolks up slowly.

straining the mixture

Use a fine mesh strainer (at least as fine as a tea strainer) to sieve the mixture just before it is to be poured into the ramekins. One helpful tip is to sieve it into a measuring cup or bowl that has a pour spout. This will make it very simple to then fill the ramekins. If you don't have a vessel that pours well, a small ladle works well.

making special brûlée sugar

It is possible to use only granulated sugar to caramelize the top of a crème brûlée, but some cooks believe that a deeper caramel color and flavor is achieved by making a special 50/50 mixture of light brown sugar and granulated sugar. With the special brûlée sugar it is possible to caramelize a thinner layer and still end up with a deeper flavor than if only white sugar were used. However, for the sugar to caramelize properly, it must be very dry. To make the mixture you will need:

1 cup light brown sugar, firmly packed
1 cup granulated sugar

Spread the light brown sugar on baking parchment on a cookie sheet or jelly roll pan. Place in a low oven (about 200° F) for at least 35 minutes or until it becomes very crisp and crumbly. Remove from oven and cool completely to room temperature. Rub chunks of the dried sugar through a coarse strainer until as much of it as possible is finely sieved. Mix the dried brown sugar with the granulated sugar and store in an airtight container. As it will not spoil, it will be ready for several batches of crème brûlée whenever you should happen to want to use it.

caramelizing the crème brûlée sugar

The surface area of the ramekin (some are smaller across and taller; others are wide and shallow) will determine how much sugar you will use, and so will your own personal taste. It is possible to create a continuous, brittle sheet of caramelized sugar using anywhere from 1 teaspoon to 1 tablespoon per 4-ounce ramekin.

As for the procedure, always torch sugar on cold custards that have just been removed from the refrigerator. Sprinkle on the sugar as evenly as possible. After following directions for lighting the torch, use the constant-on button and try to achieve a distance from the flame tip and the sugar that allows for fairly rapid melting without sudden darkening. The caramelizing should be gradual. To make this go smoothly, keep the torch moving in quick small, spiraling circles. The finished brittle surface should be light amber to medium dark amber in color. Of course, using more sugar will provide a thicker crust. This you can adjust to your own taste as you continue to make more brûlée desserts.

Cooks who do not have torches, of course, have the option of caramelizing (brûléeing) a sugar coating under the broiler. This method has never been totally satisfactory, however. An evenly crystallized coating is hard to achieve, and the broiler often overcooks the custards during this second heating. For this reason, if you must use the broiler, try to arrange the ramekins in a pan filled with ice.

classic *crème brûlée* (type I)

With this baked type, hands-on preparation time is astonishingly short, averaging only 5 to 10 minutes. Contrast between the cool, creamy custard and the crisp, warm caramelized sugar is classically superb.

1 cup whipping cream

2 egg yolks

⅓ cup sugar

Pinch of salt

½ teaspoon vanilla

6 to 8 teaspoons special brûlée sugar (page 8) or regular granulated sugar

Preheat oven to 300° F. Put cream in saucepan and stir over medium heat, just to the point of boiling. Set aside.

In small bowl, whisk the egg yolks, sugar, and vanilla until blended. Into this, add the hot cream a little bit at a time, whisking as you go until all is incorporated. Strain the mixture through a fine sieve. Place 4 (4-ounce) ramekins in a hot water bath (page 8), and fill them evenly. Bake for about 35 minutes. Custards should be mostly set, but the centers should still jiggle slightly. Remove hot water bath from oven and cool until ramekins are comfortable enough to handle. Cover with clear wrap and refrigerate at least one and a half hours or as long as two days.

Just before serving, evenly sprinkle 1 to 2 teaspoons of special brûlée sugar on the surface of each custard and torch until caramelized.

Serves 4

cook's notes: For those that prefer a less sweet custard, it is possible to cut the sugar back to ¼ cup without making any other adjustments.

classic infused *crème brûlée* (type II)

This infused, Vanilla-Bean Crème Brûlée is the mother of so many variations. Create your own essences from your favorite spices, herbs, fruits, etc. Heat them with the cream and then allow to steep until it cools. Substitute the vanilla bean for other sensuous options offered below.

½ cup whole milk

1½ cups heavy
    whipping cream

⅔ cup granulated sugar

Pinch of salt

1 vanilla bean
    (Tahitian if possible), split
    lengthwise and scrape out
    seeds — use all

6 egg yolks, from large eggs

¼ cup (generous) brûlée
    sugar (page 8) or
    regular granulated sugar

Combine the milk, cream, sugar, salt, and vanilla bean in a small saucepan and stir over medium heat until it reaches the boiling point. Set aside to steep until it cools down.

Preheat oven to 300° F, and adjust a rack slightly lower than center.

In a separate bowl, whisk the egg yolks briefly. Add the cream mixture very slowly into the yolks, whisking well with each addition. Once blended, strain the mixture through a fine sieve. Pour the custard mix evenly into 8 (4-ounce) shallow ramekins (about 1 inch high) and bake them in a water bath for 35 to 45 minutes, until centers are softly set. Remove from oven and cool in water bath until comfortable to handle. Cover the dishes and refrigerate for 2 hours. These can be stored for 1 or 2 days before serving.

To serve, sprinkle each top with about 1½ teaspoons of brûlée sugar and torch to caramelize. For thicker caramelized crunch, use more sugar. The ultimate — eating while the tops are warm and the custard is cool.

Serves **8**

variations:

Fresh Ginger Crème Brûlée • Use a generous 1-inch chunk of peeled ginger, thinly sliced.

Star Anise Crème Brûlée • Use 3 pieces of whole star anise.

Citrus Crème Brûlée • Use 1 generous tablespoon of orange or lemon zest or both, avoiding the white pith. Lime zest also produces refreshing results.

classic stovetop *crème brûlée* (type III)

This variety, involving a double boiler and gentle stirring, results in a soft, creamy, spoonable custard. It is perfect for filling pastries or hollowed-out whole fruit and is ideal for parfaits or simply as a base for cut-up mixed fruit.

Set up a double boiler at a very slow boil, making sure the top bowl does not touch the water. In the top of the double boiler, whisk the yolks, sugar, and salt, stirring occasionally. In another small saucepan, heat the cream and vanilla bean to a boil. Remove from heat and add to the yolks very slowly, whisking constantly as you drizzle it in. Continue to cook the mixture in the double boiler until it coats a wooden spoon without running off quickly (about 25 to 30 minutes). You must be patient during this time, stirring gently once in a while so that the mixture cooks evenly and does not coagulate.

When thickened, strain the mixture into a clean bowl and cool on countertop for about 10 minutes. Cover the bowl loosely, first with a paper towel and then plastic wrap over that. Move to refrigerator and chill for an additional 2 hours before using.

Serves **4**

4 **egg yolks**

4 **tablespoons white sugar**

2 **tablespoons light brown sugar, firmly packed**

Pinch of salt

1¼ **cups heavy cream**

1 **vanilla bean (at least a 4-inch segment, cut in half lengthwise)**

options: The custard can be served as a standard crème brûlée by spooning it into 4 small ramekins and caramelizing 1 to 2 teaspoons of sugar on top of each. Summer Parfait Crème Brûlée is a great application for stovetop crème brûlée (see page 16).

sugar 'n' spice *crème brûlée*

The venerable trinity of dessert flavorings — cinnamon, nutmeg, and vanilla — once again come through with a performance that deserves a standing ovation.

½ cup whole milk

1½ cups heavy whipping cream

⅔ cup granulated sugar

Pinch of salt

1 vanilla bean (Tahitian if possible), split lengthwise and scrape out seeds — use all

2 cinnamon sticks, crushed

¼ teaspoon of ground nutmeg, freshly ground if possible

6 egg yolks, from large eggs

¼ cup (generous) brûlée sugar (page 8) or regular granulated sugar

Combine the milk, cream, sugar, salt, vanilla bean, cinnamon stick, and nutmeg in a small saucepan and stir over medium heat until it reaches the boiling point. Set aside to steep the spices for about 15 minutes.

Preheat oven to 300° F, and adjust a rack slightly lower than center.

In a separate bowl, whisk the egg yolks briefly. Add the cream mixture very slowly into the yolks, whisking well with each addition. When all is blended, strain the mixture through a fine sieve. Pour the custard mix evenly into 8 (4-ounce) shallow ramekins (about 1 inch high) and bake them in a water bath for 35 to 45 minutes, until centers are softly set. Remove from oven and cool in water bath until comfortable to handle. Cover the dishes and place in the refrigerator for 2 hours to chill thoroughly. These can be stored for 1 or 2 days before serving.

To serve, sprinkle the top of each dish with about 1½ teaspoons of brûlée sugar and torch to caramelize. More sugar can be used for a thicker caramelized layer. Eating while the tops are warm and the custard is cold increases the taste sensation.

Serves **8**

summer parfait *crème brûlée*

Enticing layers of bright fruit, crème brûlée, and whipped cream fragrant with peach liqueur give high visual appeal and flavor contrast. The creamy custard provides just enough sweetness to pair perfectly with tart fresh fruit. Each glass is "capped" with amber, caramelized sugar and a few perfect berries. For this dessert you will need small parfait glasses or short-stemmed wine goblets (8 to 10 ounce).

for the brûlée:

1 recipe for stovetop, stirred crème brûlée (page 13)

½ cup blueberries (rounded), washed and dried on paper toweling

½ cup raspberries (rounded), also rinsed and gently dried off

2 medium peaches or nectarines; peeled, pitted and cut in ½-inch pieces

for the garnish (optional):

Mint sprigs, strawberry (or other fruit) slices

for the whipped cream:

1¼ cups heavy whipping cream

3 tablespoons granulated sugar

1 teaspoon peach liqueur

4 teaspoons granulated sugar (for caramelizing)

After crème brûlée is chilled and fruit and whipped cream are prepared, assemble the parfaits, layer by layer, in the following suggested manner (or one of your own design):

Begin with 2 tablespoons (generous) of brûlée custard in the bottom of the glass, then about 3 dollops of whipped cream smoothed into a second layer. You may need to use moistened paper toweling or tissue to wipe nice edges against the glass and to clean off smudges. Next, stand fruit against the glass edge, alternating blueberries and raspberries, later filling in the middle of the layer. Then another layer of whipped cream, followed by a generous layer of diced peaches. Another thin layer of whipped cream, and then top off the glass (flush with top) with 2 more generous tablespoons of custard. Cover with wrap and chill until ready to use. Can be prepared 10 to 12 hours before serving.

Just before taking to table, use a torch to caramelize 1 teaspoon of granulated sugar on the surface of each dessert. Keep the circle of sugar about ¼ inch away from the glass edge, and when torching, direct the flame more toward the center, so as not to overheat the cold glass and cause cracking. Finish with a few pieces of fresh fruit and mint along one side of the top. Another garnish option: Slices of strawberries, oranges, etc. can be hung on the edge of the glass if you cut slits in them.

Serves **4**

light 'n' breezy *crème brûlée*

This brûlée weighs in with just half the calories of the traditional one made with cream. The great thing is that nothing is lost in taste. In fact, this one has a distinct character all its own that mirrors the authentic Spanish flan and Crème Caramel. You will want to try this one simply for variety's sake.

Preheat oven to 300° F. Arrange 4 (4-ounce) shallow ramekins in a pan large enough for a hot water bath.

Combine evaporated milk, cream, and cinnamon stick in a saucepan. Stir over medium heat to the boiling point (about 2 to 3 minutes total). Allow to cool for at least 10 minutes.

In a small mixing bowl, whisk the yolks, sugar, vanilla, and salt until smooth, briskly stirring rather than beating. Drizzle in the milk mixture, stirring constantly. Blend well, strain through a fine sieve, and pour the mixture evenly into the ramekins. Bake in the hot water bath for about 35 minutes. When done, the centers should jiggle slightly when shaken. Remove from the oven and allow to cool in the water. When almost room temperature, transfer the ramekins to the fridge, covering them with wrap, and chill for at least 2 hours.

When ready to serve, sprinkle the surface of each custard with 1 teaspoon of brûlée sugar. Torch until caramelized.

Serves **4**

¾ cup 2% evaporated milk

¼ cup cream

1 cinnamon stick, crushed

3 egg yolks

3 tablespoons granulated sugar

¼ teaspoon vanilla

4 teaspoons brûlée sugar (page 8)

piña colada *crème brûlée*

The coconut cream imparts a subtle but real coconut flavor that will speak to you like a tropical breeze. Like daisies, the pineapple-garnished tops also hint at easy-going days on a sun-kissed beach.

5 egg yolks

½ cup granulated sugar

1 cup coconut cream, canned

2 tablespoons rum liqueur with natural coconut flavor

2 pinches of salt

¾ cup heavy cream

½ cup pineapple tidbits or 4 pineapple rings, canned

8 raspberries or blueberries

4 to 6 teaspoons of brûlée sugar (page 8)

Preheat oven to 300° F. Arrange 8 (4-ounce) ramekins in a pan large enough for a hot water bath.

Put 5 yolks in a small mixing bowl. Add sugar and mix vigorously with a whisk. Continue by blending in the coconut cream, liqueur, and salt.

In a saucepan, heat the heavy cream to the point of boiling, stirring often. Then pouring in a very thin stream, add it to the yolk mixture while whisking constantly. Strain the mixture through a fine sieve and then fill the ramekins evenly. Add very hot tap water to the hot water bath until it reaches about half way up the sides of the ramekins. Bake for about 40 to 45 minutes. When done, only the centers should jiggle ever so slightly. Remove hot water bath from the oven and allow the desserts to cool in the water. When comfortable enough to handle, transfer them to the refrigerator and cover loosely. Chill about 2 hours.

At serving time, drain pineapple well and dry it between paper toweling. If using pineapple rings, cut them into ¾-inch tidbits. Arrange five or six of the tidbits in a daisy shape on top of each custard. Leave space at the center of each "flower" to place a berry. Sprinkle brûlée sugar only on the pineapple petals and torch to caramelize. Serve as soon as possible.

SERVES 8

cook's notes: If more caramelizing is desired, torch a thin layer of sugar over the entire surface before arranging the pineapple. Then caramelize sugar on top of each pineapple "petal."

orange praline _crème brûlée_

Caramel sauce at the bottom with Grand Marnier flavored praline crunch on the top, and all that is silky in between.

Preheat oven to 300° F. Put 1 teaspoon of brûlée sugar into the bottom of each 4-ounce ramekin. Using the shallow, oval ramekins is preferred. Torch the sugar until it caramelizes and adheres to the ramekins.

Measure cream into small saucepan. Grate the orange zest, add to the cream, and heat while stirring, just to the point of boiling. Set aside.

In a mixing bowl, mix the egg yolks, ¼ cup of sugar, salt, and 1 teaspoon of Grand Marnier until well blended. Begin adding the hot cream to the yolk mixture in very small amounts, whisking continually until both are blended. Strain the mixture through a fine sieve.

Pour the cream and yolk mixture into the ramekins evenly. Place them in a hot water bath (page 6) and bake for about 35 minutes, until the custard jiggles only slightly in the centers. Remove from oven and allow to cool in the water bath. Then cover each with wrap and refrigerate for at least an hour before serving.

To prepare for serving, put the pecans in a cup and pour 1 tablespoon of Grand Marnier over them, mixing to wet all surfaces. Pour the brûlée sugar on a small plate. Caramelize nuts as directed below.

Whip the cream with the 2 teaspoons of granulated sugar in a small bowl. Pipe decoratively around the outer edge of the custard. Arrange the praline pieces in the center of each dessert and serve.

Serves **4**

for the brûlée:

4 teaspoons special brûlée sugar (page 8) or granulated sugar

1 cup cream

1 tablespoon orange zest

3 egg yolks

¼ cup granulated sugar

Pinch of salt

1 teaspoon Grand Marnier

for the topping:

12 pecan halves

1 tablespoon Grand Marnier

½ cup brûlée sugar

⅓ cup whipping cream

2 teaspoons granulated sugar

caramelizing pecans: Roll the pecan pieces, one at a time to coat with sugar. Place the pieces on an inverted stainless steel cake pan. Torch them to caramelize. If thicker coating is desired, sprinkle more sugar on them at any time and keep torching. Turn the pieces over and sprinkle with more sugar and torch. Allow to cool completely. Cut into smaller pieces if desired.

double deep
chocolate *crème brûlée*

A silky hybrid of dark chocolate ganache and bittersweet pots de crème. A hint of caramel sauce forms naturally during the baking to complement the chocolate and add one more layer of dreaminess.

4 teaspoons brûlée sugar (page 8) or regular granulated sugar

2 squares unsweetened baking chocolate (2 ounces)

1 cup heavy cream

2 egg yolks

⅓ cup plus 2 tablespoons granulated sugar

Pinch of cinnamon

Pinch of salt

½ teaspoon vanilla

Butter for greasing ramekins

Preheat oven to 300° F. You will need 4 (4-ounce) custard cups or ramekins that are at least 1½ inches deep. Sprinkle 1 teaspoon of brûlée sugar evenly on the bottom of each cup and torch until caramelized.

Put the chocolate squares and the cream in a small double boiler or saucepan on low heat. Whisk the two together as melting occurs. As soon as the chocolate is mostly melted, add the ⅓ cup plus 2 tablespoons of sugar and continue to whisk well. This will bring the cream and the chocolate together into a very smooth mixture. Remove from heat.

In another small mixing bowl, mix the egg yolks, cinnamon, salt, and vanilla until blended. Then add the chocolate cream to the egg yolk mixture, about one-third at a time, whisking well with each addition.

Grease only the sides of the ramekins and fill them evenly with the chocolate mixture. Place the cups in a hot water bath (page 6) and bake for 35 to 40 minutes (centers should be softly set). Take out of oven and cool briefly in the bath. When able to handle, take them out and chill for at least 2 hours if you plan to unmold the desserts. Another option is to serve them at room temperature. You can refrigerate for up to 2 days if you desire to make them ahead.

When serving, unmolded custards should be placed on dessert plates with good color contrast and they can be served as is. They can also be left in the cups and topped with whipped cream and a few pinches of cocoa powder. Another option is to top each with a dollop of marshmallow cream and torch it lightly for a roasted marshmallow flavor.

SERVES **4**

white chocolate
raspberry *crème brûlée*

This extra creamy, dreamy brûlée has many variations (see below). It can make use of jams and fruits that you have on hand. Buying a high quality white chocolate like Callebaut or using a brand you know to be good will give you results that will meet your expectations.

Preheat oven to 300° F. You will need 4 tall, round (4-ounce) ramekins. Spread generous ½ tablespoon jam in the center bottom of each cup. Set aside.

Melt the white chocolate in the cream in a small saucepan over very low heat. Keep stirring to blend until most melting is accomplished. Then add ¼ cup sugar immediately and whisk gently until all is dissolved and mixture is smooth. Remove from heat.

In another small mixing bowl, mix egg yolks, salt, and vanilla about 1 minute until blended. Next, add the white chocolate cream to the egg yolk mixture, a little at a time, whisking well with each addition to make sure the heat is distributed gradually. Strain with a fine sieve.

Gently ladle the cream mixture into each ramekin, distributing evenly. Place the cups in a hot water bath (page 6) and bake 35 to 40 minutes or until centers jiggle ever so slightly. Take out of oven and cool in the bath to room temperature. Then cover and refrigerate for at least 2 hours or up to 2 days before serving.

To prepare for serving, sprinkle about 1½ teaspoons of brûlée sugar on the surface of the custard. Torch the sugar until caramelized. Arrange 4 raspberries, perhaps stacking one on top of three others to give a little height. Add mint leaves if desired and serve promptly.

Serves **4**

2½ tablespoons all-fruit raspberry jam

4 ounces chopped white chocolate or almond bark

¾ cup heavy cream

¼ cup milk

3 egg yolks

¼ cup granulated sugar

Pinch of salt

½ teaspoon vanilla

16 fresh raspberries

6 teaspoons special brûlée sugar (page 8) or regular granulated sugar, for caramelizing

Mint leaves (optional) for garnish

variation: The exact same process can be used to make brûlée with other all-fruit jams (homemade or commercial) strawberry, blueberry, prickly pear cactus, etc. Use your imagination and then try to top with a fresh fruit of the same theme. When ready to serve, sprinkle with sugar. Caramelize as directed.

option: A little sugar can also be caramelized over the raspberries.

espresso *crème brûlée*

This may not replace your morning coffee, but some have been known to have it for breakfast. It's fun to make this one, over and over, using different coffees for different effects. Happy experimenting!

2 tablespoons double espresso or very strong coffee (see below)

¾ cup heavy cream

3 egg yolks

⅓ cup sugar

¼ teaspoon vanilla

1 tablespoon Kahlua or Kamora (or other coffee liqueur)

4 teaspoons brûlée sugar (page 8) or granulated sugar

Whipped cream (for garnishing), optional

Coffee bean candies (for garnishing), optional

Use your favorite coffee and make very strong espresso if you have an espresso machine. If not, use a drip filter system and pour ¼ cup boiling water over 3 generous tablespoons of finely ground coffee. If time permits, you can run the coffee through the same grounds two times. Let it drip slowly and cool. You will use only 2 tablespoons for the recipe.

Stirring in a saucepan, heat the cream just to the boiling point. Set aside.

In a small mixing bowl, combine the egg yolks, sugar, vanilla, coffee liqueur, and lukewarm strong coffee. Whisking continually, add the hot cream into the egg yolk mixture in very small amounts, blending well with each addition until both are combined.

Pass the mixture through a fine sieve. Pour or ladle into 4 (4-ounce) ramekins. Place them in a hot water bath (page 6) and bake for 35 minutes if shallow, oval ramekins are used. For taller ramekins, 40 minutes or more may be needed. Remove from oven and allow to cool about 10 minutes in the water bath before refrigerating. Chill covered for about 2 hours before serving.

To prepare for serving, sprinkle about 1 teaspoon of brûlée sugar on the surface and torch until caramelized. If so desired, whipped cream and coffee bean candies can be used to decorate.

Serves **4**

variation: This can also be done as an infused brûlée. Instead of using liquid coffee, barely grind about ¼ cup of your favorite beans. Mix the ground coffee into 1 cup of cream (instead of ¾ cup) and heat to boiling. Allow to cool for at least 10 minutes. Proceed as directed in all other regards.

snappy apple *crème brûlée*

To intensify the flavor and decrease unwanted moisture, dried apples are used. The snap comes from plumping the apples in Grand Marnier, and the nuts provide a welcome touch of crunch. If you prefer fresh apples, begin with at least ¼ cup and cook down to evaporate moisture.

Measure milk and cream into saucepan. Add broken-up cinnamon sticks and stir while heating, just until boiling. Set aside to cool.

Preheat oven to 300° F. Get out 4 (4-ounce) custard cups and a cake pan large enough for a hot water bath (page 6).

Combine chopped apple, Grand Marnier, water, and cinnamon in small saucepan. Stir, cover, and cook slowly until plumped. Set aside to cool.

In a small mixing bowl, whisk together the egg, egg yolks, ¼ cup sugar, and salt with a brisk stirring motion, rather than beating, to prevent too many air bubbles. Add the cream mixture to the egg mixture, little by little, until blended and sugar is dissolved. Strain through a fine sieve into a pour spout cup or bowl.

Mix the walnuts well with the plumped apple bits. Divide the apple and walnut mixture evenly in the bottoms of the 4 custard cups. Press down slightly. Spoon 1 teaspoon of brûlée sugar on top of the apple bits and torch to caramelize. Slowly pour the cream mixture over the top of the apples in each cup until distributed evenly. The apples may or may not float to the top. Do not worry about this. Place cups in hot water bath and bake for about 40 minutes (centers should have very little jiggle). Remove from hot water, cool nearly to room temperature, and then refrigerate for at least 2 hours.

If unmolding to serve, turn upside down and simply garnish with a touch of crème fraiche and a sprinkling of cinnamon. Another option is to serve them in the cups. If doing so, sprinkle 1 teaspoon of brûlée sugar on top of each custard in a circle only around the edge and caramelize it with a torch. Then add a small dollop of crème fraiche in the center and sprinkle with cinnamon. This provides an extra bit of caramel crunch if served immediately.

Serves 4

- ¾ cup heavy cream
- ¼ cup milk
- 2 cinnamon sticks
- ⅓ cup dried apple bits, ⅛-inch pieces
- 1 tablespoon Grand Marnier
- 1 tablespoon water
- ¼ teaspoon cinnamon
- 1 egg
- 3 egg yolks
- ¼ cup granulated sugar
- Pinch of salt
- ⅛ cup chopped walnuts
- 8 teaspoons of brûlée sugar (page 8) or granulated sugar

peanut butter
fudge *crème brûlée*

This two-tone delicacy has the earmark of a true-blue, all-American brûlée. Get ready to see what happens when peanut butter goes to finishing school.

¼ cup creamy peanut butter

¼ cup sugar

1 egg yolk

¼ teaspoon vanilla

½ cup hot fudge ice cream topping

¾ cup cream

for the topping:

3 tablespoons marshmallow crème

2 teaspoons cream

1 generous teaspoon peanut butter

Preheat oven to 300° F. In a quart mixing bowl, combine peanut butter, egg yolk, sugar, and vanilla. As you stir, the mixture will grow thicker and harder. Set aside.

Prepare 4 (4-ounce) ramekins by spreading about 2 tablespoons of hot fudge in the bottom of each. The hot fudge sauce should be at room temperature.

In a saucepan over medium heat, stir cream and bring to boiling point. Pour the cream in very small amounts and work it into the peanut butter mixture using a heavy spoon. It will be difficult at first, but little by little you can begin to use a whisk. When the mixture is smoothly blended, pour it through a fine strainer to remove all coarse material. Fill ramekins and bake, using a hot water bath (page 6), for about 35 to 45 minutes (35 for shallow ramekins, 45 for taller ones) or until centers are softly set. Remove from the water bath and cool on a rack for 15 minutes before putting in the refrigerator. Chill for about 2 hours.

To serve, thoroughly mix topping ingredients with a spoon. Spread evenly on top of each and torch until lightly browned.

Serves 4

cranberry-
vanilla *crème brûlée*

As cream goes beautifully with any tart fresh fruit, so it is, too, with cranberries. In some recipes cranberries are thought of as "the poor relative," the cheap substitute for fresh cherries, etc. However, in this brûlée, they take center stage and bring the house down.

Preheat oven to 300° F. Put whole cranberry sauce and 2 tablespoons sugar in small saucepan and cook for 15 minutes on medium heat to reduce all moisture. Stir often to prevent scorching. Put one generous tablespoon of the cooked sauce in each of 4 shallow (4-ounce) ramekins. Try to put at least 6 whole berries in each ramekin.

In another small saucepan, heat cream with ¼ cup sugar to the boiling point. Set aside. In a small bowl, whisk the egg yolks and the vanilla. Add in the hot cream in small amounts, whisking continually. Pour the mixture through a fine strainer. Ladle the mixture gently over the berries. Place the full ramekins in a hot water bath (page 6). Bake for 30 minutes on a rack just a little lower than the middle of the oven. When done, the centers should still jiggle ever so slightly. Remove from oven, cool slightly, and remove from bath. When cool enough to handle, cover with wrap and chill for at least 2 hours.

When ready to serve, sprinkle a generous teaspoon of brûlée sugar over the surface and torch until evenly caramelized.

Serves **4**

⅔ cup whole berry cranberry
   sauce, canned (select
   as many whole berries
   as possible)

2 tablespoons sugar

1 cup heavy cream

¼ cup granulated sugar

2 egg yolks

½ teaspoon vanilla

4-5 teaspoons brûlée sugar
   (page 8), for caramelizing

s'more *crème brûlée*

An American picnic favorite and French artistry shake hands to form a brûlée that's just waiting to make an appearance at your next patio party.

1 **cup regular whipping cream**

3 **egg yolks**

¼ **cup granulated sugar**

1 **teaspoon vanilla**

Pinch of salt

2 **graham crackers,
(2¼ x 6 inches)**

1 **tablespoon butter**

2 **tablespoons finely chopped
walnuts or pecans
(optional)**

1 **thin Hershey's milk
chocolate candy bar**

1 **small jar marshmallow
crème**

Preheat oven to 300° F. Measure the 1 cup of cream into a small saucepan and stir over low heat, just to the boiling point. Set aside.

In a small mixing bowl, stir together the egg yolks, sugar, vanilla, and salt until well blended and fairly smooth. Do not whip.

Add the warmed cream into the egg mixture, little by little, stirring well during each addition, until both are completely blended. Pour the mixture through a fine strainer. Lightly butter 4 round, tall ramekins (4-ounce). Place them in a hot water bath (page 6) and fill each evenly with the custard mixture. Bake for 40 to 45 minutes.

Remove from the water bath and cool to room temperature. Cover with wrap and chill in the refrigerator from 2 hours to 2 days before using.

When ready to serve, preheat oven to 375° F. Cut each graham cracker into two squares and lightly brush both sides with butter, distribute pieces of the candy bar on top of all four pieces, place on a baking sheet and heat for 10 minutes in the oven. While these are heating, chop the nuts.

To assemble the desserts, place a chocolate-covered cracker on each dessert plate and unmold a chilled custard on top of it. Sprinkle with nuts and then top with dollop of marshmallow crème. Torch the marshmallow crème until a light golden crust forms. Serve immediately.

Serves **4**

milk chocolate *crème caramel*

Your spoon will unfold the drama, gliding through the golden silk custard and finally reaching the luscious chocolate chunks and amber caramel sauce waiting at the bottom. Hard to believe the preparation time is just ten minutes.

Preheat oven to 300°F. You will need 4 (4-ounce ramekins) — choose the tall type if you plan to unmold the desserts to feature the caramel. Prepare a hot water bath (page 6).

Divide brûlée sugar evenly among the ramekins. Torch the sugar until the bottom of each cup is completely caramelized; some of the sugar may turn the color of molasses. Place chocolate pieces on top of caramel and heat dishes in oven for 3 minutes. Set aside.

In a saucepan over low heat, scald the milk and cream together just until bubbles begin to form. Do not over boil it.

In another small bowl, whisk the egg yolks with the white sugar and vanilla, just until well blended. No need to beat. Then add small amounts of the hot cream mixture, stirring well with each addition until all is blended. Pour the mixture back into the measuring cup through a fine strainer.

Place the ramekins in hot water bath. Slowly pour the cream mixture evenly over the chocolate and caramelized sugar. Carefully place the baking pan on an oven shelf slightly lower than the center of the oven. Bake until centers are softly set, still jiggling slightly when shaken, usually 35 to 40 minutes, depending on the shape of the ramekins.

Remove pan from the oven, taking care not to splash any water onto the custards. Cool almost to room temperature in the bath. Then take out, cover with clear wrap and chill in the refrigerator for at least 1 hour.

If you choose to serve with garnish, try a fine dusting of cocoa powder, piped whipped cream, caramelized nuts (page 23), milk chocolate curls, mint leaves, or crispy cookies. See unmolding tips on page 44.

Serves 4

6 teaspoons brûlée sugar (page 8)

1 ounce milk chocolate pieces

¼ cup milk

¾ cup heavy cream

3 egg yolks

¼ cup granulated sugar

½ teaspoon vanilla

Butter for greasing

eggnog *crème brûlée*

It's bound to conjure up images of Christmases past, but don't limit this one to the holidays. The most heart-warming, with brandy or rum, takes no more time than the non-alcoholic version.

¾ cup heavy cream

¼ cup milk

¼ teaspoon freshly grated nutmeg

3 egg yolks

⅓ cup sugar

½ teaspoon vanilla

Pinch of salt

for the topping:

⅔ cup marshmallow crème

2 tablespoons heavy cream

Pinch of nutmeg

1 teaspoon brûlée sugar (page 8)

Preheat oven to 300° F. In a small saucepan, heat the cream, milk, and ¼ teaspoon of nutmeg together until very hot but not boiling. Set aside and allow the spice to steep for 5 to 10 minutes. In the meantime, combine the egg yolks, sugar, vanilla, and salt in a small mixing bowl, stirring vigorously for about 30 seconds. No need to whip.

Next, add the cream mixture to the egg yolks in small amounts, whisking constantly until both are smoothly blended. Strain the mixture through a fine sieve. Fill 4 tall, round ramekins (4-ounce) with the mixture. Place in a hot water bath (page 6) and bake about 50 minutes or until centers barely jiggle. Take out of oven and allow to cool in the bath until comfortable to handle. Then cover with wrap and refrigerate for about 2 hours before serving. Can be made 2 days in advance.

To serve, prepare the topping by combining the marshmallow crème and heavy whipping cream with a generous pinch of ground nutmeg. Whisk until smooth. Spread the topping evenly over the surface of the brûlée and then sprinkle on brûlée sugar very sparingly (about ¼ teaspoon). Torch until surface is caramelized to a light golden brown. Serve as soon as possible.

Serves **4**

rum or brandy variation: In the topping, replace one tablespoon of the heavy cream with one tablespoon of your favorite rum or brandy.

banana split *crème brûlée*

True, it's a miniature version, but this proves that great things can come in small packages. The rich brûlée custard replaces the customary ice cream to create a praise-winning combination of caramelized bananas, milk chocolate ganache, cherries, whipped cream, and nuts for those that love them.

Make the Crème Brûlée custard of your choice, using 4-ounce shallow, oval ramekins, and chill as directed, but do not caramelize the top.

To make the ganache, put the ¼ cup cream and chocolate pieces in a small saucepan and heat on low just until the chocolate is melted. Remove from heat and whisk until smooth. Cool to room temperature or chill if thicker is desired, and it's ready to use.

Combine the three ingredients for the whipped cream and whip to stiff peaks. Set aside.

Slice the bananas into ¼-inch rounds. Halve the cherries, removing pits. Chop the nuts as desired.

Stack 7 banana slices, like dominoes, from end to end across the center of each ramekin. Pour 1 teaspoon of brûlée sugar right down the middle of each banana row. Torch to caramelize. Arrange 2 cherry halves at the ends on both sides. Spoon ganache on both sides of the bananas or drizzle at will. Pipe or spoon whipped cream in mounds along the perimeter. If so desired, it is possible to put the whipped cream along the edge before drizzling the chocolate ganache. Cherry pieces on each end and a sprinkle of nuts should finish them off nicely.

Serves 4

1 recipe Classic Brûlée (I), (II), or (III), pages 10, 12, or 13 respectively

for the ganache:

3 to 3½ ounces milk chocolate

¼ cup heavy cream

for the whipped cream:

½ cup heavy cream

1 tablespoon sugar

⅛ teaspoon vanilla

2 bananas

8 fresh Bing cherries, halved and pitted (or sweet black cherries, canned)

8 walnut or pecan halves, chopped

4 teaspoons special brûlée sugar

upside-down *crème brûlée*

This reverse process brûlée is most commonly known as Spanish Flan or Crème Caramel. Once unmolded, a caramel syrup bathes the silky custard. It is best to use the taller, round 4-ounce ramekins so the custards stand higher when turned out.

¼ cup granulated sugar, (plus 4 teaspoons for caramelizing)

1 cup half 'n' half

2 egg yolks

1 egg

¾ teaspoon vanilla

Pinch of salt

You will need 4 deep, 4-ounce custard cups or ramekins. Sprinkle one teaspoon of sugar in the bottom of each ramekin and caramelize with a torch, moving the flame in slow spirals, until amber or dark amber beads form over the entire bottom surface. Set aside to cool.

Preheat oven to 300° F. Combine ¼ cup sugar and half 'n' half in a saucepan. Stir well while heating until almost to the boiling point. Set aside.

In another bowl, briskly stir the egg yolks, whole egg, vanilla, and salt, without beating, until very liquid. Try not to create too many bubbles. Continuing to stir briskly, add the cream mixture slowly in a thin stream until all is blended. Strain the mixture through a fine sieve and fill the ramekins, taking care to pour gently. Place in a hot water bath (page 6) and bake about 40 minutes until the centers are softly set. They should jiggle slightly. Remove the hot water bath from oven and allow the custards to cool in the water for about 10 minutes. When comfortable enough to handle, cover the ramekins with wrap and chill in the refrigerator for about 2 hours. Unmold (see tip below) and serve.

Serves 4

unmolding tip for serving: Hold the bottom two-thirds of each ramekin in a bowl of hot tap water for a count of 20. Then, with a small paring knife, go around the edge of each custard. Turn the ramekin over in the center of the dessert plate. If the custard does not fall out, gently slip the paring knife along one side. This will release the vacuum and the custard will come out.

garnish suggestions: Rosettes of whipped cream and fresh raspberries provide a wonderful palette of contrasting colors and flavors. Chocolate curls, candied citrus peel or cinnamon and cocoa sprinklings can add a natural paired dimension to the caramel.

mellow
pumpkin *crème brûlée*

Pumpkin pie, move over! The smoothness you'll experience in this brûlée is rare in pumpkin desserts and the spices are designed to be subtle. Start a new Thanksgiving tradition.

Preheat oven to 300° F. In small mixing bowl, combine all of the ingredients except for the heavy cream. Stir the pumpkin mixture with a small whisk or spoon for a full minute. Set aside.

Put the heavy cream in a saucepan and stir while heating, just to the point of boiling. Whisk the hot cream into the pumpkin mixture in small amounts until all is blended, stirring for a full minute.

Pour the mixture through a fine strainer into another bowl or large measuring cup. Place 4 (4-ounce) shallow ramekins in a hot water bath (page 6). Fill with the pumpkin mixture and place on an oven rack slightly below the middle of the oven. Bake for 35 to 40 minutes or less if centers are softly set.

Cool the ramekins in the hot water bath until comfortable to handle. Then cover with wrap and refrigerate from 1 hour to 2 days before using. When ready to serve, remove from fridge and sprinkle 1½ teaspoons of sugar on each ramekin and torch to caramelize.

Serve immediately.

Serves **4**

¼ cup pumpkin

¼ cup sour cream

3 egg yolks

¼ cup light brown sugar, firmly packed

2 tablespoons granulated sugar

⅛ teaspoon allspice

⅛ teaspoon cinnamon

Generous pinch of nutmeg (fresh ground if possible)

Pinch of salt

½ cup heavy cream

6 teaspoons special brûlée sugar (page 8) or granulated sugar, for caramelizing

beyond crème brûlée:
creative uses for the cooking torch

Quickly toast a **mini-marshmallow topping** on any sweet potato casserole or dessert.

Ever try broiled grapefruit? It's one way to make this Vitamin C-rich fruit more popular on your breakfast table: Halve cold or room temperature fruit crosswise and loosen the sections. Dab the surface dry with a paper towel. Spread on a little soft butter. Sprinkle with cinnamon and then a thin layer of sugar. Torch until all sugar is bubbly and melted. Serve as soon as possible.

Melting cheese is a snap:

- Perhaps this is the time to try a wonderful onion gratinée soup.
- On a relish tray, stuffed celery logs look and taste great when thin strips of any natural cheese is laid across the top and torched until bubbly.
- Melted and browned grated cheese is also wonderful as a finishing touch for cooked fish fillets.
- Did all the cheese disappear on your scalloped potatoes or casserole as it baked? Just add a little more cheese and torch until golden and bubbly.

Add a lightly browned crust to **brown sugar-based frostings** containing nuts and coconut.

Create magical, glassy "butterflies" for cake decoration by crystallizing the surface of miniature or standard-sized **orange slice candies** or other similar gelled candies with white sugar coatings. Cut the candies in half through the centers, place on a heat-proof surface and torch until glassy.

Lightly brown a **buttered breadcrumb** and **parmesan cheese topping** for stuffed tomatoes or avocado-halve salads. This type of "crust" can also be added to the top of cooked fish fillets.

Browning meringues (all stovetop cooked types or those made with pasteurized egg whites or those that have been heated to at least 145° F for 15 seconds): For example, "Randy's Chantilly Meringue" (page 71) or Swiss meringue (a divinity type).

Warming and flaming liqueur or liquor: Place the needed liqueur or liquor in a stainless steel measuring cup and warm the bottom of it with the flame of the torch. The liquor does not have to be super hot. Then pour the alcohol onto the fruit or dish you want to flame and light it with the torch.

Quick-roasting peppers and tomatoes: Create the same effect as oven-broiling or roasting in just minutes. Once the outside of the pepper or tomato is charred, put in a covered dish until cooled. Then peel off the skin and use as needed.

Caramelizing Sugar for Various Dishes:

- Glazing Ham after it has been cooked: Fruit can be laid on the surface and all sprinkled with granulated or special brûlée sugar (page 8) before torching to caramelize.
- Caramelizing nuts: A simple method for creating pralines is given on page 23. This same process will work for other nuts as well. To dampen the nuts before rolling in sugar, you can substitute fruit juice or wine for liqueur if it is more convenient.
- Brûléed Fresh Fruit makes a unique topper for all types of pudding, ice cream, cake, and rich custard. Pour a thin layer of granulated or special brûlée sugar (page 8) on the fruit and torch until it becomes glazed.
- Caramelized sugar decorations: On smooth foil that has been placed on a heat-proof surface (such as an inverted cake pan), granulated sugar can be sprinkled about one-eighth-inch deep in a variety of shapes or lines. After torching and making sure all sugar is melted, the caramelized sugar can be peeled from the foil. Discs, coils, zigzag sticks, straight sticks, etc. can be created. These thin sugar sculptures can then be used as finishing touches to top a variety of desserts.
- Rolled, cream-filled crepes get a wonderful finish with a light glassy coating of caramelized sugar.

brûléed
hazelnut cream *tart*

The ever so smooth hazelnut cream filling is nestled between a nutty, crisp crust and a caramelized top. To prepare for this recipe, 4 ounces (1 rounded cup) of hazelnuts should be roasted on a baking pan at 350° F for 10 minutes. Using a clean hot pad or small towel, roll or rub the nuts while hot to remove most of the skins. Additional rubbing can be done when they are cool. When cooled, the skins can be discarded. Hazelnuts (also called filberts) can be found in the nut section of most grocery stores.

for the crusts:

Set aside 10 roasted hazelnuts to be used later for garnish. In a food processor, chop 1 cup of toasted hazelnuts as finely as possible. Measure out ¼ cup to be used in the crust, and reserve ¾ cup for the filling. Begin preparing one recipe for Sweet Tart Crust. After creaming the butter and sugar, add ¼ cup of the finely chopped hazelnuts just before adding the flour. Finish mixing as directed. Note Tip for Rolling also on page 53. Bake crust at 350° F for 20 to 25 minutes, until golden in color. Remove from oven and set aside.

(continued next page)

for the crust: (use a removable bottom 9-inch tart pan, if possible)

1 cup roasted hazelnuts (to be divided for crust, filling, and garnish)

1 recipe of Sweet Tart Crust (page 53)

(continued from previous page)

brûléed hazelnut cream *tart*

for the filling:

½ cup whole milk

¾ cup finely chopped roasted hazelnuts (reserved while making crust)

1½ cups cream

⅔ cup firmly packed light brown sugar

3 tablespoons cornstarch

⅛ teaspoon salt

4 egg yolks

¼ teaspoon vanilla

5 teaspoons brûlée sugar (page 8)

10 toasted hazelnuts (reserved for garnish)

for the whipped cream:

½ cup cream

2 tablespoons sugar

for the filling:

In blender, purée ¾ cup finely ground hazelnuts with the milk. Add ½ cup of the cream also, in small amounts, to help the mixture move in the blender. Continue processing one more minute. At lower speed, add the remaining cream, light brown sugar, cornstarch, and salt. When mixture is smooth, add the egg yolks and vanilla and blend briefly. Pour the mixture into a heavy saucepan (nonstick is best) and, stirring slowly, bring to a boil over medium heat. Stir and boil for one additional minute. Pour the thickened filling into a small mixer bowl, cover, and allow to cool to room temperature.

To assemble the tart, whip the ½ cup cream with 2 tablespoons sugar until firm peaks form. With low speed beater, fluff up the hazelnut filling, and then, with a spatula, fold in half of the whipped cream. Reserve the other half of the whipped cream to use later for decorating the top. Pour the filling into the baked crust and smooth the surface. Refrigerate for about 2 hours.

When almost ready to serve, sprinkle the brûlée sugar from the center to within an inch of the crust edge. With torch, caramelize this circle of sugar. In the open space around the edge, pipe or spoon the reserved whipped cream in small mounds or rosettes. Further garnish with halved hazelnuts. Portions will cut better before removing the tart from the pan.

Serves **8** to **10**

"**black bottom" variation:** For the chocolate lovers, 3 ounces of chopped milk chocolate can be spread and melted on the crust bottom as soon as it is taken from the oven. After coating the bottom with chocolate, cool completely before adding the filling. All other aspects of the recipe remain the same. For garnish, consider shaved chocolate curls. If desired, meringue can be used instead of whipped cream.

topping option: Do concentric circles of caramelized sugar and meringue (page 71). Use the torch to brown the meringue. Also garnish with more hazelnuts.

sour cream-
raisin meringue *tart*

This hybrid draws upon a popular Midwest pie filling, a classic European sweet tart crust, and a New York presentation. And for the sake of the cook, the tart dough uses a mixer process that takes only minutes. Double-wrapped dough freezes well one month.

for the crust:

With a hand-held mixer in small mixer bowl, whip butter 1 minute on high speed. Add sugar and vanilla, continuing to cream at least one more minute. Then, on lowest speed, add in the flour until crumbles form (10 seconds). Again, on low speed, add water to form small clumps (5 seconds). Stop mixing immediately, press the dough into a ball, put in a gallon-sized zip-lock bag and flatten into a disc. Refrigerate at least 30 minutes. When ready to use, leave on the counter until just soft enough to roll (See tip below). Let the crust rest in the pan (at least 20 minutes) until the oven is heated. Preheat oven to 350° F. Bake on center rack for 10 to 15 minutes or until slightly golden. Remove from oven. It is now ready to fill.

(continued next page)

for the sweet tart crust:
(for a 9-inch tart pan)

¾ **stick of room-temperature salted butter (6 table-spoons)**

3 **tablespoons sugar**

¼ **teaspoon vanilla**

1 **cup all-purpose flour (fill the cup lightly, spoonful by spoonful)**

2 **teaspoons ice water**

tip for rolling: Roll the dough right in the zip-lock bag, until it extends to the very edges. Cut away one side of the bag and place dough-side down into the tart pan. Peel away the remaining plastic and ease the crust into all creases. Redistribute pieces of dough until all edges are even. Cracks can easily be removed by pressing and forming the dough with your fingers. Prick sides and bottom, every inch, with a fork.

(continued from previous page)

sour cream-raisin meringue *tart*

for the sour cream-raisin filling:

½ cup granulated sugar

½ cup firmly packed light brown sugar

2 tablespoons flour

Dash of salt

2 cups sour cream

½ teaspoon vanilla

¾ cup raisins, whole or slightly chopped

3 egg yolks

for the filling:

In a heavy saucepan, combine the first 4 dry ingredients; then add sour cream, vanilla, and raisins, blending well. Cook over medium heat, stirring often. Lightly whisk egg yolks in small mixing bowl. When stovetop mixture is bubbling strongly, add some into the egg yolks and whisk briskly. Then add the egg yolks back into the boiling filling, whisking vigorously while incorporating. Continue to boil and stir the mixture for an additional minute or two. Remove from heat and pour into the baked tart shell.

When ready to serve, prepare Randy's Chantilly Meringue (page 71). Pipe or spoon it onto the filling in cloud-like balls or swirls. Avoid skinny peaks as they burn easily. Torch until covered with beautiful golden highlights. This meringue also bakes well at 350° F for about 12 minutes. Can be served at room temperature.

Serves 8 to 10

fresh fruit
chantilly crowns

Simplicity, seasonal freshness, and elegant meringue come together to make fruit something special, regardless of the time of year. Although mango, blueberries, strawberries, and kiwi are featured here, the very same eye-appeal and flavor concert can be accomplished with winter citrus, bananas, and candied cranberries. Coconut and nuts also go well with many fruit combinations and can be added as desired.

In a bowl, mix all of the fruit with the 3 tablespoons of sugar and the Grand Marnier. Cover with wrap and keep chilled, stirring occasionally. This should be done at least 20 minutes before serving, and no longer than 2 hours.

As the fruit marinates, prepare the meringue as directed. Once stiff peaks are achieved, prepare the "crowns" within 15 minutes or so. On each individual dessert plate or in shallow 5-inch ramekins, create a ring of meringue that is about 1 inch wide with at least a 3-inch open center. The ring can be created by dropping dollops from a spoon, or by piping with a pastry bag. Using a grooved tip will create more interest. To make the ring higher, pipe or spoon a second layer. Each ring nest should stand at least 2 inches high. Using a torch, brown the meringue lightly from all sides. The meringue crowns can be made about 1 hour before serving, if necessary. Let stand without covering.

To serve, fill the rings high with fresh fruit and divide the juice evenly among them. Garnish with mint leaves and take to the table as soon as possible.

Serves 4

1 mango, about 3 inches in diameter, peeled and cut in ½-inch cubes

½ pound of strawberries, in ¼-inch slices

½ cup blueberries, whole

1 kiwi, peeled and cut in ½-inch pieces

3 tablespoons granulated sugar

1 tablespoon Grand Marnier or other fruity liqueurs, (optional)

Sprigs of fresh mint for garnish, (optional)

1 recipe for Randy's Chantilly Meringue (page 71)

cook's notes: This meringue is also great for pies and tarts. It was specially developed to be torched, browns easily and dramatically, while holding its shape and whipped cream quality.

baked alaska

Few would think of this as a make-ahead dessert, but it almost is. A half-gallon carton of ice cream is easy to store. The rich, supple cake stays exceedingly moist for up to two days if covered with wrap. Even most of the assembling can be done several hours before guests arrive. The cake-covered igloo of ice cream does well in the freezer for a few hours. Making the meringue, however, should be done the hour before guests arrive (15 minutes). Right before serving, there's spreading on the meringue and torching it (10 minutes at most). Voila! A long-time favorite that never fails to impress.

for the butter fudge cake:

2⅓ cups brown sugar, firmly packed

2¼ cups all-purpose flour (fluff it with a spoon when measuring)

1½ teaspoons baking soda

½ teaspoon baking powder

½ teaspoon cinnamon

⅛ teaspoon salt

3 ounces unsweetened baking chocolate, cut in pieces

½ cup salted butter (1 stick), at room temperature

1 cup sour cream

3 eggs, separated (large or extra large)

½ teaspoon vanilla

1 cup room temperature water

Preheat oven to 350° F, and arrange a rack in the center or just slightly below center of the oven. Prepare an 11 x 17-inch sheet pan (12 x 18 is fine) by greasing and lining with baking parchment. It is best to grease one side of the paper and then flip it over and do the other side as well.

In large mixer bowl, combine the first 6 ingredients.

In a small microwave-safe bowl, heat the chocolate in ½ minute intervals, stirring until well melted. There is no need to overheat. Set aside.

Add the butter and sour cream to the dry ingredients and mix well at low speed until mostly blended. Stop the mixer and separate the eggs. Put the whites in a small mixer bowl and add the yolks and the melted chocolate to the batter. Mix the batter at medium speed until smooth, and then at high speed for an additional minute.

With a separate hand mixer, whip the egg whites to fairly firm peak stage. Set aside.

Add the vanilla to the batter bowl, begin beating on low speed and add in water at a very slow drizzle until smoothly blended. Do not overbeat. Last of all, remove bowl from mixer and with a rubber spatula, add a large dollop of the batter to the egg whites and fold it until blended. Now pour the egg white mixture into the large batter bowl and fold all of it over and over until fully incorporated. Pour batter into baking pan, smoothing the surface. Bake for 30 minutes, or slightly longer, until the center feels firm and a toothpick inserted tests clean of raw batter. Cool the cake in the pan for at least an hour and up to 2 days if covering with plastic wrap after it reaches room temperature. *(continued next page)*

(continued from previous page)

baked alaska

for the ice cream center:

½ gallon vanilla-based ice cream (or ice milk) containing bits of cookie, chocolate, etc.

for the meringue:

Double recipe of Randy's Chantilly Meringue (page 71)

It is very important to double the amount of all ingredients (6 egg whites, etc.), even though procedure is the same.

for the assembly:

You will need a cake platter that is larger than 9 inches. Exactly in one corner of the sheet pan, cut a 9-inch circle of cake (using a pie plate or round cake pan as a guide). Peel carefully from parchment and place it in the center of the platter.

Cut the carton away from the ice cream. With sharp knife, cut a two-inch section off one end of the block. Stand the remaining block in the center of the cake circle. Cut the 2-inch section in half lengthwise and stand each piece on the wide sides of the big block. The object is to create an igloo shape, so, using a spoon and knife, carve away square edges along the top and fill in roundly and smoothly along the sides, being sure to leave a 1-inch edge of cake exposed around the bottom.

Next, cut trapezoidal shaped sections of cake that are about 7 inches long, 2 inches wide at the top, and 3 inches wide at the bottom. Press these against the side of the ice cream all around until the igloo is completely covered. You will need to cut a very small circle or odd shaped pieces of cake to fill in the very top and any large cracks between segments. Refreeze the cake and ice cream from 20 minutes to 2 hours while you prepare the meringue and get ready to serve it.

When ready to serve, spread the meringue in swirls (or pipe it on with a pastry bag) working from the bottom up. Swirls and rounded shapes will highlight better with a torch than peaks will. Torch the meringue so that golden or light brown highlights cover the entire surface. Serve immediately. Cut with a long, thin knife that has been dipped in warm water. Wipe the knife and re-dip as each new piece is cut.

Serves **10** to **12**

cook's note: This version obviously favors the chocolate lover; the contrast between layers is extremely stunning and important to consider. You can, however, use any of your favorite moist cakes and ice creams, keeping in mind that, ideally, there should be a darker layer between two lighter portions, or at least a strong gradation of color.

tip: Did the beautiful stiff peaks of your meringue fizzle before you got around to spreading it on the cake? No need to panic. The meringue recommended here for this dessert can be re-beaten on the mixer at high speed and it will come back to stiff peaks wonderfully. Three cheers for fail-safe!

option: Quarter-inch pieces of walnuts or pecans can be poked into the ice cream after it is formed into the igloo shape, just before sections of cake are formed over it.

crème brûlée
apricot kuchen

Kuchen was perhaps the original deep dish fruit pizza. It has always featured a thin custard filling, so it is a natural step to go all the way and make it a crème brûlée custard. Since kuchen is not extremely sweet, the extra caramelization adds a hint more flavor, sweetness, and texture, all at the same time. Wonderful for a brunch or dessert.

for the dough:

In a small saucepan, heat the milk until slightly warmer than body temperature. Remove from heat and mix in the yeast. Pour the milk mixture into a large mixing bowl and use the same saucepan to melt the butter. Set aside.

In a small bowl, beat the eggs and whisk in the sugar, sour cream, salt, and nutmeg. Add the egg mixture and melted butter to the milk and yeast, mixing well.

Next, whisk in 2 cups of flour and continue to stir for about 2 minutes. Add in another cup of flour and, with heavy spoon, stir for at least 1 more minute. Add remaining flour and bring the dough together into a medium stiff ball. On countertop, knead for 5 to 10 minutes until smooth. Place back in bowl, cover, and place in warm place for about 1 ½ hours (dough should double in size). While dough is proofing, prepare the filling.

(continued next page)

for the dough:

¾ cup warm milk

1 package dry yeast

½ cup melted butter

2 beaten eggs,
   room temperature

½ cup sugar

½ cup sour cream,
   room temperature

½ teaspoon salt

¼ teaspoon nutmeg, freshly
   ground if possible

4¾ cups all-purpose flour

(continued from previous page)

crème brûlée apricot kuchen

for the filling:

In small saucepan, whisk cream and cornstarch until blended. Stirring, heat the cream until it becomes uncomfortable to the touch. Set aside. In a small mixing bowl, beat the eggs with the ⅔ cup sugar, liqueur, and salt. Pour the cream into the egg mixture, whisking continually until both are well blended. Mix in cottage cheese. Set aside.

When dough has doubled, divide in two equal portions and roll or press each portion into a 12-inch square on two sheet cake pans. When forming the dough in the pans, be sure to create a slightly raised edge against the sides, so middle can hold filling. If too high, the edge will be too "bready" when baked. Cover and allow to rise for half an hour.

Ladle in the cream and cheese mixture evenly. Place apricot pieces in a pattern or randomly. With your fingers, sprinkle about ¼ teaspoon of cinnamon over the surface of each kuchen. Preheat oven to 350° F. Allow kuchens to rise a bit more on countertop while oven is heating. Bake for about 30 minutes. Custard should be set quite firmly. Remove from oven and cool to room temperature. Before serving, distribute caramelizing sugar on top of custard portion and torch it, being careful not to direct the flame at the bread along the edge. After baking, kuchen freezes well for a couple weeks if double wrapped, but caramelizing should be done after thawing.

Serves 18

for the filling:

1½ cups heavy cream

2 teaspoons cornstarch

4 egg yolks

⅔ cup sugar

3 tablespoons peach liqueur

2 pinches of salt

¾ cup full-fat cottage cheese

1½ cups fresh apricots, sliced or chunked (½ inch); canned apricots may also be used if well drained

½ teaspoon cinnamon

6 tablespoons brûlée sugar (page 8) or granulated sugar (for caramelizing top)

cook's notes: If round kuchens cut in wedges are preferred, divide the dough in 3 portions and press the dough into 3 greased, round 9-inch cake pans, creating a slight edge. Finish as directed. Baking time may vary slightly. When done, the custard at the very center may still jiggle ever so slightly.

variations: This cheese kuchen is equally fine with sliced peaches, lightly fried apple slices, raspberries, plums or mixed fruit. If fruit is very tart, you may increase the sugar in the filling by a couple of tablespoons.

lemon cream tartlets with chantilly meringue

Isn't every grandmother known for her lemon meringue pie? These tartlets will help to preserve the popularity of creamy lemon for all posterity. Rather than ordinary pie crust, a sweet tart dough is used. A touch of cream makes the filling extra smooth, while the cloud-soft Chantilly Meringue browns up dramatically.

for the crust:
Sweet Tart Crust (page 53)

for the lemon cream filling:
Juice of one large lemon, (generous ¼ cup)

Zest of one large lemon, (about 1 tablespoon lightly packed; avoid using the white pith)

¾ cup water

½ cup plus 2 tablespoons granulated sugar

2 tablespoons salted butter

3 tablespoons cornstarch dissolved in 2 tablespoons of cold water

¼ cup cream

3 egg yolks (reserve the 3 egg whites for the meringue)

for the meringue:
Randy's Chantilly Meringue

crust for the tartlets:

Prepare one recipe of Sweet Tart Crust (page 53). Shallow ramekins or tartlet forms of your choice can be used to bake the crust. Bake the crusts prior to making the filling and meringue, so the lemon custard can be poured directly into the shells when it is ready.

lemon cream filling:

In a medium saucepan, combine the lemon juice, zest, ¾ cup of water, sugar, and butter, and bring to a boil. In the meantime, dissolve the cornstarch in 2 tablespoons of cold water, add the cream and egg yolks and whisk until smooth. When the lemon mixture boils, remove it from the heat briefly, and whisking constantly, pour in the creamy egg mixture slowly until all is blended. Return to medium heat and continue whisking gently for about 5 minutes, making sure the filling has returned to a bubbly boil and is well thickened. Fill tart shells immediately if they are ready. Otherwise, the filling can be left in the pan, lightly covered, to cool at room temperature.

meringue:

Using the 3 reserved egg whites, make one recipe of Randy's Chantilly Meringue (page 71). Pipe or spoon the meringue on top of filled tarts. Filling can be hot or cooled. Torch for beautiful dramatic highlights or bake meringue-topped tarts for 12 minutes at 350° F. Remove tartlets from forms and serve at room temperature or lightly chilled.

Makes at least 6 (4-inch tarts) or more if smaller tart forms are used.

"brûléed"
new york cheesecake

Present the most classic cheesecake with unique flair. Each slice is "brûléed" just before serving, giving a "glassy," classy finish. A final garnish of fresh or candied fruit add the perfect point of color.

Preheat oven to 350° F. Prepare a 7- or 8-inch springform pan by greasing lightly with butter. Process the grahams in food processor until finely crushed. Measure the crumbs and put back in processor with butter, sugar, and cinnamon. Pulse until well mixed. If any lumps of butter remain, rub the mixture with your fingers until well blended. Press the crust mixture evenly on the sides and bottom of the pan. It is sometimes helpful to put a thin plastic bag or wrap over your hand as you do this. The bottom of a glass works to firm the bottom part of the crust. Bake 10 minutes, remove from oven, and set aside.

In large mixer bowl, whip the cream cheese, sour cream, sugar and Grand Marnier on high speed for 1 to 2 minutes. Add eggs one at a time, beating well with each addition. Lastly, mix in the zest only until blended. Pour batter into the prebaked crust. Reduce the oven temperature to 300° F and bake for 1 hour. Turn off oven and leave until pan is comfortable to handle without potholders. Take out, cover loosely and chill for 2 hours.

Many people believe cheesecake tastes better close to room temperature. Before serving, mix sour cream and cinnamon for topping. With a knife, mark lines in the top of the cake where the wedges will be cut. With a warm, slightly wet knife, make straight cuts all the way through the cake until desired wedges are achieved. Clean and rewet the knife between cuts. Remove the side of the springform. Spread the topping evenly. Sprinkle generous ½ teaspoon of brûlée sugar over the surface of each wedge. Torch the sugar to caramelize. Place strawberry slices, candied citrus peel, or candied fruit along the crust edge.

Serves 8 to 10

for the crust:

1⅓ cups graham cracker crumbs (about 9 grahams; 4-inch x 8-inch pieces)

2 tablespoons butter, at room temperature

1½ tablespoons sugar

⅛ teaspoon cinnamon

for the cake:

1 pound cream cheese

⅓ cup sour cream

½ cup granulated sugar

1 tablespoon Grand Marnier or Cointreau

3 eggs

Zest of one lemon, finely grated

for the topping:

¼ cup sour cream

⅛ teaspoon cinnamon

5 to 6 teaspoons brûlée sugar (page 8) or granulated sugar, for caramelizing

Sliced strawberries or candied fruit for garnish

crackling filled pears

When these anise and cinnamon-infused pears finish baking, they get finished off with crème filling and brûléed "top hats." A great way to "spice up" fall and winter fruit.

1 recipe of Classic Brûlée (III), (page 13, can be made 1 or 2 days in advance)

4 ripe pears (Bartlett or Bosc)

¼ cup light brown sugar

2 tablespoons butter

4 cinnamon sticks

4 pieces whole star anise

¼ cup orange marmalade

½ cup finely chopped walnuts, toasted

2 tablespoons pear brandy or Galliano liqueur (optional)

Make the basic stirred crème brûlée as directed. Refrigerate for at least 2 hours.

Preheat oven to 350° F. Leaving the stem and top of neck intact, peel the pears. With melon baller, scoop out the seed core from the bottom.

Blend the brown sugar and butter and stuff it into the scooped-out cavity of each pear. Then imbed one cinnamon stick and anise piece deep into the center of the butter filling.

Place the pears, standing, in a small baking pan or dish. Reserve half of the marmalade and smear the remaining portion on the peeled surface of the pears. Bake uncovered for 20 to 30 minutes.

While the pears are baking, toast the walnuts in a frying pan over medium high heat. Stir continually. When starting to smell browned, pour immediately onto a cool plate to stop the toasting. Roasting should be very subtle.

Remove baked pears from the pan to a plate, cover, and chill for 1 hour. To the syrup in the baking pan, add ⅓ cup water and 2 tablespoons liqueur, boiling gently to reduce to a spoonable sauce.

When ready to serve the desserts, assemble as follows: Remove all spices remaining in the pear cavity. (These can be used later to garnish the plates.) Fill each pear with brûlée custard, brush more marmalade on the bottom half and roll in the nuts. Stand on individual dessert plates and cut off the top inch of each pear. Spread one additional spoon of custard on the cut surface. Pour 1 teaspoon of brûlée sugar (page 8) on the custard-covered top. Torch to caramelize. Drizzle liqueur sauce around each pear, and garnish with whole spices and serve.

Serves 4

⚬ cook's notes: Baking apples substitute well for pears, but must be baked covered just until tender crisp, not mushy. Toasted ground almonds can be used in place of walnuts. Baked type crème brûlée can also be spooned into the centers.

randy's chantilly *meringue*

This meringue has been specially developed to have a whipped cream texture, not to be overly sweet, to hold up well, and to produce dramatic browning effects with a culinary torch. Perhaps even more importantly, a heating method is used to remove fear of salmonella infection. Last but not least, the quantities and method used in this recipe produce no-fail results every time, with a truly stiff meringue that pipes or spoons equally well.

You can use this meringue on any crème brûlée custard base. Occasionally, in place of the traditional caramelized sugar coating, a creamy meringue gives a pleasant change of pace.

Mix all ingredients in the top of a double boiler. Keep stirring (do not beat) with a spoon or whisk until the temperature of the whites comes to 145° F. Hold this temperature for 15 seconds, then remove top of double boiler immediately and transfer the contents to a large mixer bowl. Then with mixer on high speed, whip the mixture continually until truly stiff peaks form. This process usually takes 5 minutes, more or less, and will be accomplished as the mixture cools near to room temperature.

3 egg whites

6 tablespoons granulated sugar

¼ teaspoon cream of tartar

⅛ teaspoon vanilla

cook's notes: This meringue whips equally as well if pasteurized eggs are used (then heating is unnecessary). The heating step can also be eliminated if dried egg whites are used and reconstituted according to package directions.

Meringue should not be left at room temperature for more than 2 hours. Unused meringue can be stored, covered in the refrigerator for up to a day. It may liquefy slightly at the bottom of the bowl as it stands for lengths of time. In this case, only use the top, stiffer portion.

Meringue on filled pies and brûlées can be baked or torched. If baking is preferred, use a 350-degree oven for 12 minutes on a middle rack.

SEVERAL RECIPES IN THIS BOOK UTILIZE THIS MERINGUE. CHECK THEM OUT:

fresh fruit chantilly crowns, *page 57* • sour cream-raisin meringue tart, *page 53*
baked alaska, *page 58* • lemon cream tartlets, *page 64*
brûléed hazelnut cream tart, *page 51*

index

about the author

Randolph Mann's love for cooking began as a childhood romance and his passion for creating in the kitchen shows no signs of abating. Formal training for this chef began in earnest at the Sheraton in South Seattle during the Woodstock era. Always fueled by challenge, he went on to get involved in the successful opening of the Red Fox, an experimental seafood restaurant in Bellevue, Washington, and then some years later, an upscale dinner club called Sir Patricks in the Heartland.

In 1986, doors opened for him to teach at a national university in Japan. For ten years, the author devoted himself to the fine details of Asian cuisine, became an expert gardener and herbalist, and then opened a cooking school where "East meets West" proved to be a big hit. Randolph and his daughter Kelsey Lane, a graduate of California Culinary Academy, have pooled their passion for food and gardening to produce a definitive cookbook, due out in 2004, for avid container gardeners. Now back in the States, the author works as a cookbook author and editor with Silverback Books of San Francisco. He is currently head pastry chef and baker for the Hotel Donaldson, a boutique hotel in Fargo, North Dakota.

copyright and credits

Text and original recipes created by: **Randolph Mann**

Design, Art Direction and Layout by **Platinum Design, Inc. NYC**

Photography by **Lisa Keenan**

Food Stylist: **Agnes (Pouke) Halpern**

Props courtesy of **Sur La Table**

Stockfood: photo on pages 2-3

FoodPix: photos on inside front cover, page 7, and page 18

The BonJour name and logo are the property of BonJour, Inc.

ISBN 1-930603-97-5

Printed in China